Hear Our Prayer

An Anthology of Classic Prayers

A LION BOOK

Text compiled by Olivia Warburton

A Lion Book
an imprint of
Lion Hudson plc
Mayfield House, 256 Banbury Road,
Oxford OX2 7DH, England
www.lionhudson.com
ISBN 0 7459 4856 1

First edition 2005
10 9 8 7 6 5 4 3 2 1 0

Acknowledgments: See page 128

A catalogue record for this book is available
from the British Library

Typeset in 9/12 Americana
Printed and bound in Singapore

Lord, make me an instrument of thy peace:
where there is hatred, let me sow love;
where there is injury, pardon;
where there is discord, union;
where there is doubt, faith;
where there is despair, hope;
where there is darkness, light.

ATTRIBUTED TO ST FRANCIS OF ASSISI

Contents

SEEKING GOD   11

PRAISE   23

THANKSGIVING   35

CONFESSION   43

PETITION   51

INTERCESSION   63

Morning and Evening   71

The Church Year   83

Church Rites   103

Graces and Blessings   115

Index of Authors   122

Index of First Lines   123

Introduction

Prayer, the church's banquet, angel's age,
God's breath in man returning to his birth,
The soul in paraphrase, heart in pilgrimage,
The Christian plummet sounding heaven and earth.
Engine against the Almighty, sinner's tower,
Reversèd thunder, Christ-side-piercing spear,
The six-days world transposing in an hour,
A kind of tune, which all things hear and fear;

Softness, and peace, and joy, and love, and bliss,
Exalted manna, gladness of the best,
Heaven in ordinary, man well dressed,
The milky way, the bird of Paradise,
Church bells beyond the stars heard, the soul's blood,
The land of spices; something understood.

George Herbert

AS I WONDERED how best to introduce this book,
I found myself turning to a seventeenth-century
English religious poet for inspiration. George Herbert's
poem 'Prayer' is a brilliant sketch of some of the
things prayer can be. In what seems almost to be
a carelessly flung together collection of word-pictures,
and through images ranging from the familiar to the
mystical, he offers something that draws us into the
whole concept of what prayer is and should be.

Far from being a set of dry words, prayer is 'the
church's banquet', through which we feast and are
filled. 'God's breath in man returning to his birth' is
a beautiful summary of how God gives us the breath
of life and how through prayer we can in a sense
return that breath to him. Later in the sonnet Herbert
introduces a similar idea in referring to 'exalted manna'
– the heavenly food that God sent down on his exiled
people returning to the sender.

And then again, prayer can 'sound' the distance
between heaven and earth. In another of his poems,
Herbert says,
'The heavens are not too high,
His praise may thither fly:
The earth is not too low,
His praises there may grow.'
In both prayer and praise the distance between God
and man can be bridged.

Prayer is what happens when our heart is 'in pilgrimage'. It can, Herbert admits, be something terrible, misused, something that wounds the heart of God. Yet it is also 'softness, and peace, and joy, and love, and bliss', transcendent experiences and qualities; what Herbert calls 'heaven in ordinary' – ordinary people glimpsing heaven as they pray.

In its closing lines the sonnet moves into increasingly exotic imagery: 'The milky way... the bird of Paradise... church bells beyond the stars heard... the land of spices...' before coming to rest in a breathtakingly simple statement of what prayer to our heavenly Father ultimately is: 'something understood'.

Olivia Warburton

Seeking God

Lord, teach me to seek you,
and reveal yourself to me
as I look for you.

ST AMBROSE OF MILAN

As a deer longs for flowing streams,
so my soul longs for you, O God.
My soul thirsts for God, for the living God.
When shall I come and behold the face of God?
My tears have been my food day and night,
while people say to me continually,
'Where is your God?'

These things I remember,
as I pour out my soul:
how I went with the throng,
and led them in procession to the house of God,
with glad shouts and songs of thanksgiving,
a multitude keeping festival.
Why are you cast down, O my soul,
and why are you disquieted within me?
Hope in God; for I shall again praise him,
my help and my God.

Psalm 42

Eternal Trinity, you are a deep sea,
into which the more I enter the more I find,
and the more I find the more I seek.

The soul ever hungers in your abyss, Eternal Trinity,
longing to see you with the light of your light,
and as the deer yearns for the springs of water,
so my soul yearns to see you in truth.

St Catherine of Siena

O God, you are my God,
  earnestly I seek you;
my soul thirsts for you,
my body longs for you,
in a dry and weary land
where there is no water.

I have seen you in the sanctuary
and beheld your power and your glory.
Because your love is better than life,
my lips will glorify you.
I will praise you as long as I live,
and in your name I will lift up my hands.
My soul will be satisfied as with the richest of foods;
with singing lips my mouth will praise you.

On my bed I remember you;
I think of you through the watches of the night.
Because you are my help,
I sing in the shadow of your wings.

Psalm 63: 1–7

O gracious and holy Father,
  give us wisdom to perceive you,
intelligence to understand you,
diligence to seek you,
patience to wait for you,
eyes to behold you,
a heart to meditate upon you,
and a life to proclaim you,
through the power of the Spirit
of our Lord Jesus Christ.

Attributed to St Benedict of Nursia

O God, you are the light of the minds that know you,
the life of the souls that love you,
and the strength of the wills that serve you:
help us so to know you that we may truly love you,
and so to love you that we may fully serve you,
whom to serve is perfect freedom;
through Jesus Christ our Lord.

St Augustine of Hippo

God, of your goodness,
give me yourself,
for you are sufficient for me.
To be worthy of you
I cannot ask for anything less.
If I were to ask less,
I should always be in want,
for in you alone do I have all.

Julian of Norwich

O Lord, the Scripture says,
'There is a time for silence,
and a time for speech.'
Saviour, teach me
the silence of humility,
the silence of wisdom,
the silence of love,
the silence of perfection,
the silence that speaks without words,
the silence of faith.
Lord, teach me to silence my own heart
that I may listen to the gentle movement
of the Holy Spirit within me
and sense the depths which are of God.

Frankfurt prayer, sixteenth century

My dearest Lord,
be thou a bright flame before me,
a guiding star above me,
a smooth path beneath me,
a kindly shepherd behind me,
today and for evermore.

St Columba of Iona

Agreeing to lose everything for you, O Christ,
in order to take hold of you,
as you have already taken hold of us,
means abandoning ourselves to the living God.
Centring our life on you, Christ Jesus,
means daring to choose:
leaving ourselves behind so as no longer to walk
on two roads at the same time:
saying no to all that keeps us from following you,
and yes to all that brings us closer to you,
and through you, to those whom you entrust to us.

Brother Roger of Taizé

O Father, give my spirit power to climb
to the fountain of all light, and be purified.
Break through the mists of earth, the weight of clay,
shine forth in splendour, you who are calm weather
and quiet resting place for faithful souls.
You carry us, and you go before;
you are the journey, and the journey's end.

Boethius

L ord Jesus Christ, you said that you are
  the Way, the Truth, and the Life;
let us never stray from you, who are the Way;
nor distrust you, who are the Truth;
nor rest in any other but you, who are the Life,
beyond whom there is nothing to be desired,
either in heaven or on earth.
We ask it for your name's sake.

Desiderius Erasmus

I bind unto myself today
  the power of God to hold and lead,
his eye to watch, his might to stay,
his ear to hearken to my need.
The wisdom of my God to teach,
his hand to guide, his shield to ward;
the Word of God to give me speech,
his heavenly host to be my guard.

Christ be with me, Christ within me,
Christ behind me, Christ before me,
Christ beside me, Christ to win me,
Christ to comfort and restore me.
Christ beneath me, Christ above me,
Christ in quiet, Christ in danger,
Christ in hearts of all that love me,
Christ in mouth of friend and stranger.

Attributed to St Patrick of Ireland, translated Mary Byrne and Eleanor Hull

L ord, teach me to seek you,
  and reveal yourself to me as I look for you.
For I cannot seek you unless first you teach me,
nor find you unless first you reveal yourself to me.

St Ambrose of Milan

Lord, take as your right,
and receive as my gift,
all my freedom, my memory,
my understanding and my will.
Whatever I am and whatever I possess,
you have given it to me;
I restore it all to you again,
to be at your disposal,
according to your will.
Give me only a love for you,
and the gift of your grace;
then I am rich enough,
and ask for nothing more.

St Ignatius Loyola

My Father,
I abandon myself into your hands.
Do with me as you will.
Whatever you may do with me,
I thank you.
I am prepared for anything,
I accept everything,
provided your will is fulfilled in me
and in all creatures.
I ask for nothing more, my God.
I place my soul in your hands,
I give it to you, my God,
with all the love of my heart,
because I love you.
And for me it is a necessity of love,
this gift of myself,
this placing of myself in your hands,
in boundless confidence,
because you are my Father.

Charles de Foucauld

O make my heart so still, so still,
When I am deep in prayer,
That I might hear the white mist-wreaths
Losing themselves in air!

Utsonomya San

A ll is silent.
In the still and soundless air,
I fervently bow
to my almighty God.

Hsieh Ping-hsin

O my divine Master,
teach me to hold myself in silence before you,
to adore you in the depths of my being,
to wait upon you always
and never to ask anything of you
but the fulfilment of your will.
Teach me to let you act in my soul,
and form in it the simple prayer
that says little but includes everything.
Grant me this favour
for the glory of your name.

Père Grou

L ord Jesus, I am not an eagle.
All I have are the eyes and the heart of one.
In spite of my littleness,
I dare to gaze at the sun of love,
and I long to fly towards it.

St Thérèse of Lisieux

O Lord, you have searched me
and you know me.
You know when I sit and when I rise;
you perceive my thoughts from afar.
You discern my going out and my lying down;
you are familiar with all my ways.
Before a word is on my tongue
you know it completely, O Lord.
You hem me in – behind and before;
you have laid your hand upon me.
Such knowledge is too wonderful for me,
too lofty for me to attain.

Psalm 139:1–6

As the hand is made for holding
and the eye for seeing,
you have fashioned me, O Lord, for joy.
Share with me the vision to find that joy everywhere:
in the wild violet's beauty, in the lark's melody,
in the face of a steadfast man, in a child's smile,
in a mother's love, in the purity of Jesus.

Scottish Celtic prayer

O Divine Master, grant that I may not so much seek
to be consoled as to console;
to be understood as to understand;
to be loved as to love;
for it is in giving that we receive,
it is in pardoning that we are pardoned,
and it is in dying that we are born to eternal life.

Attributed to St Francis of Assisi

Praise

Let all the world
in every corner sing,
My God and King!

GEORGE HERBERT

May none of God's wonderful works keep silence,
night or morning.
Bright stars, high mountains, the depths of the seas,
sources of rushing rivers:
may all these break into song as we sing
to Father, Son and Holy Spirit.
May all the angels in the heavens reply: Amen! Amen! Amen!
Power, praise, honour, eternal glory to God, the only giver of grace.
Amen! Amen! Amen!

Third-century hymn

I believe, O Lord and God of the peoples,
that thou art the creator of the high heavens,
that thou art the creator of the skies above,
that thou art the creator of the oceans below.
I believe, O Lord and God of the peoples,
that thou art he who created my soul and set its warp,
who created my body from dust and from ashes,
who gave to my body breath,
and to my soul its possession.

Carmina Gadelica

If my lips could sing as many songs
as there are waves in the sea:
if my tongue could sing as many hymns
as there are ocean billows:
if my mouth filled the whole firmament with praise:
if my face shone like the sun and moon together:
if my hands were to hover in the sky like powerful eagles
and my feet ran across mountains as swiftly as the deer;
all that would not be enough to pay you fitting tribute,
O Lord my God.

Jewish prayer

Glorious Lord, I give you greeting!
Let the church and chancel praise you,
let the plain and the hillside praise you,
let the dark and daylight praise you,
let the birds and the honeybees praise you,
let the male and the female praise you,
and I shall praise you, Lord of glory:
glorious Lord, I give you greeting!

Welsh prayer

Praise the Lord.
Praise the Lord from the heavens,
praise him in the heights above.
Praise him, all his angels,
praise him, all his heavenly hosts.
Praise him, sun and moon,
praise him, all you shining stars.
Praise him, you highest heavens
and you waters above the skies.
Let them praise the name of the Lord,
for he commanded and they were created.
He set them in place for ever and ever;
he gave a decree that will never pass away.

Praise the Lord from the earth,
you great sea creatures and all ocean depths,
lightning and hail, snow and clouds,
stormy winds that do his bidding,
you mountains and all hills,
fruit trees and all cedars,
wild animals and all cattle,
small creatures and flying birds.

Let them praise the name of the Lord,
for his name alone is exalted.

Psalm 148:1–10, 13

Most high, most powerful, good Lord,
to you belong praise, glory, honour and all blessing!

Praised be my Lord God with all his creatures,
and especially our brother the sun,
who brings us the day and brings us the light:
fair is he and shines with a great splendour.
O Lord, he signifies you.

Praised be my Lord for our sister the moon,
and for the stars,
which he has set clear and lovely in the heavens.

Praised be my Lord for our brother the wind,
and for air and cloud, calms and all weather,
by which you uphold life in all creatures.

Praised be my Lord for our sister water,
who is very serviceable unto us
and humble and precious and pure.

Praised be my Lord for our brother fire,
through whom you give light in the darkness;
and he is bright and pleasant and very mighty and strong.

Praised be my Lord for our mother the earth,
who sustains us and keeps us,
and brings forth various fruits and flowers of many colours.

Praise and bless the Lord, and give thanks unto him,
and serve him with great humility.

St Francis of Assisi

Let all the world in every corner sing,
'My God and King!'

The heavens are not too high,
His praise may thither fly:
The earth is not too low,
His praises there may grow.
Let all the world in every corner sing,
'My God and King!'

The church with psalms must shout,
No door can keep them out:
But, above all, the heart
Must bear the longest part.
Let all the world in every corner sing,
'My God and King!'

George Herbert

You are holy, Lord, the only God,
and your deeds are wonderful.
You are strong, you are great,
you are the most high, you are almighty.
You, Holy Father, are King of heaven and earth.
You are Three and One, Lord God, all good.
You are good, all good, supreme good,
Lord God, living and true.
You are love, you are wisdom.
You are humility, you are endurance.
You are rest, you are peace.
You are joy and gladness, you are justice and moderation.
You are all our riches, and you suffice for us.
You are beauty, you are gentleness.
You are our protector, you are our guardian and defender.
You are courage, you are our haven and hope.
You are our faith, our great consolation.
You are our eternal life, great and wonderful Lord,
God almighty, merciful Saviour.

St Francis of Assisi

I am giving thee worship
with my whole life,
I am giving thee assent
with my whole power,
I am giving thee praise
with my whole tongue,
I am giving thee honour
with my whole utterance,
I am giving thee reverence
with my whole understanding,
I am giving thee offering
with my whole thought,
I am giving thee praise
with my whole fervour,
I am giving thee humility
in the blood of the lamb.
I am giving thee love
with my whole devotion,
I am giving thee kneeling
with my whole desire,
I am giving thee love
with my whole heart,
I am giving thee affection
with my whole sense,
I am giving thee my existence
with my whole mind,
I am giving thee my soul,
O God of all gods.

Scottish prayer

Let us, with a gladsome mind,
Praise the Lord, for he is kind.
For his mercies shall endure,
Ever faithful, ever sure.

John Milton

There is no place where God is not,
wherever I go, there God is.
Now and always he upholds me with his power
and keeps me safe in his love.

Anon

Glory to the Father,
who has woven garments of glory
for the resurrection;
worship to the Son,
who was clothed in them at his rising;
thanksgiving to the Spirit,
who keeps them for all the saints;
one nature in three, to him be praise.

Syrian Orthodox Church

To God the Father, who first loved us,
and made us accepted in the beloved Son;
to God the Son, who loved us
and washed us from our sins in his own blood;
to God the Holy Spirit,
who sheds abroad the love of God in our hearts;
to the one true God be all love and all glory
for time and eternity.

Thomas Ken

To thee, O Jesu, I direct my eyes;
to thee my hands, to thee my humble knees;
to thee my heart shall offer sacrifice;
to thee my thoughts, who my thought only sees;
to thee my self – my self and all I give;
to thee I die;
to thee I only live.

Attributed to Sir Walter Raleigh

Move our hearts
with the calm, smooth flow of your grace.
Let the river of your love run through our souls.
May my soul be carried by the current of your love,
towards the wide, infinite ocean of heaven.

Gilbert of Hoyland

You, my God,
are eternal and all-powerful:
through you and in your time
the dew comes down,
the wind blows
and the rain falls.
You feed the living.
You uphold those who waver,
those torn apart by doubt,
those in anguish
and those, indeed, who risk falling into sin.
You restore the sick
and set the prisoners free;
you bring the dead back to life
according to the promise that you gave
to those who lie in darkness
in the earth.

Jewish prayer

My soul glorifies the Lord
and my spirit rejoices in God my Saviour,
for he has been mindful of the humble state of his servant.
The Mighty One has done great things for me –
holy is his name.
His mercy extends to those who fear him,
from generation to generation.
He has performed mighty deeds with his arm;
he has scattered those who are proud in their inmost thoughts.
He has brought down rulers from their thrones
but has lifted up the humble.
He has filled the hungry with good things
but has sent the rich away empty.

Luke 1:47–48, 49–53

L ord Jesus,
I give thee my hands to do thy work.
I give thee my feet to go thy way.
I give thee my eyes to see as thou seest.
I give thee my tongue to speak thy words.
I give thee my mind that thou mayest think in me.
I give thee my spirit that thou mayest pray in me.
Above all, I give thee my heart
that thou mayest love in me
thy Father, and all mankind.
I give thee my whole self
that thou mayest grow in me,
so that it is thee, Lord Jesus,
who lives and works and prays in me.
I hand over to thy care, Lord,
my soul and body,
my prayers and my hopes,
my health and my work,
my life and my death,
my parents and my family,
my friends and my neighbours,
my country and all men,
today and always.

Lancelot Andrewes

N ow thank we all our God,
With hearts and hands and voices,
Who wondrous things hath done,
In whom his world rejoices;
Who from our mothers' arms
Hath blessed us on our way
With countless gifts of love,
And still is ours today.

Martin Rinckart

Thanksgiving

O Lord, that lends me life,
Lend me a heart replete
with thankfulness.

WILLIAM SHAKESPEARE

O God, we thank you for this earth, our home;
for the wide sky and the blessed sun,
for the salt sea and the running water,
for the everlasting hills and the never-resting winds,
for trees and the common grass underfoot.
We thank you for our senses
by which we hear the songs of birds,
and see the splendour of the summer fields,
and taste of the autumn fruits,
and rejoice in the feel of the snow,
and smell the breath of the spring.
Grant us a heart wide open to all this beauty;
and save our souls from being so blind
that we pass unseeing
when even the common thornbush
is aflame with your glory,
O God our creator,
who lives and reigns for ever and ever.

Walter Rauschenbusch

I thank you, O God,
for the pleasures you have given me
through my senses;
for the glory of thunder,
for the mystery of music,
the singing of birds
and the laughter of children.
I thank you for the delights of colour,
the awe of the sunset,
the wild roses in the hedgerows,
the smile of friendship.
I thank you for the sweetness of flowers
and the scent of hay.
Truly, O Lord, the earth is full of your riches!

After Edward King

Thou that hast given so much to me,
Give one thing more, a grateful heart.
See how thy beggar works on thee
By art.

He makes thy gifts occasion more,
And says, If he in this be crossed,
All thou hast given him heretofore
Is lost.

But thou didst reckon, when at first
Thy word our hearts and hands did crave,
What it would come to at the worst
To save.

Perpetual knockings at thy door,
Tears sullying thy transparent rooms,
Gift upon gift, much would have more,
And comes.

This notwithstanding, thou wentst on,
And didst allow us all our noise:
Nay, thou hast made a sigh and groan
Thy joys.

Not that thou hast not still above
Much better tunes than groans can make;
But that these country-airs thy love
Did take.

Wherefore I cry, and cry again;
And in no quiet canst thou be,
Till I a thankful heart obtain
Of thee:

Not thankful when it pleaseth me;
As if thy blessings had spare days:
But such a heart whose pulse may be
Thy praise.

George Herbert

We thank you, O Lord and Master,
for teaching us how to pray simply and sincerely to you,
and for hearing us when we so call upon you.
We thank you for saving us from our sins and sorrows,
and for directing all our ways this day.
Lead us ever onwards to yourself;
for the sake of Jesus Christ our Lord and Saviour. Amen.

Father John of the Russian Church

Thanks be to thee, my Lord Jesus Christ,
for all the benefits thou hast won for me,
for all the pains and insults thou hast borne for me.

O most merciful Redeemer, Friend and Brother,
may I know thee more clearly,
love thee more dearly,
and follow thee more nearly,
day by day.

St Richard of Chichester

Give thanks to the Lord, for he is good;
his love endures for ever.

Open for me the gates of righteousness;
I will enter and give thanks to the Lord.
This is the gate of the Lord
through which the righteous may enter.
I will give you thanks, for you answered me;
you have become my salvation.

The stone the builders rejected
has become the capstone;
the Lord has done this,
and it is marvellous in our eyes.

Psalm 118:1, 19–23

The Lord is my shepherd,
I shall not be in want.
He makes me lie down in green pastures,
he leads me beside quiet waters,
he restores my soul.
He guides me in paths of righteousness
for his name's sake.
Even though I walk
through the valley of the shadow of death,
I will fear no evil,
for you are with me;
your rod and your staff, they comfort me.

You prepare a table before me
in the presence of my enemies.
You anoint my head with oil;
my cup overflows.
Surely goodness and love will follow me
all the days of my life,
and I will dwell in the house of the Lord
for ever.

Psalm 23

Oh, the Lord is good to me,
And so I thank the Lord,
For giving me the things I need:
The sun, the rain and the apple seed:
The Lord is good to me.

Attributed to John Chapman

O God our Father,
we would thank you for all the bright things of life.
Help us to see them,
and to count them,
and to remember them,
that our lives may flow in ceaseless praise;
for the sake of Jesus Christ our Lord.

J.H. Jowett

For summer rains, and winter's sun,
For autumn breezes crisp and sweet;
For labours doing, to be done,
And labours all complete;
For April, May, and lovely June,
For bud, and bird, and berried vine;
For joys of morning, night, and noon,
My thanks, dear Lord, are thine!

For loving friends on every side,
For children full of joyous glee;
For all the blessed heavens wide,
And for the sounding sea;
For mountains, valleys, forests deep,
For maple, oak, and lofty pine;
For rivers on their seaward sweep,
My thanks, dear Lord, are thine!

For light and air, for sun and shade,
For merry laughter and for cheer;
For music and the glad parade
Of blessings through the year;
For all the fruitful earth's increase,
For home and life, and love divine;
For hope, and faith, and perfect peace,
My thanks, dear Lord, are thine!

John Kendrick Bangs

We plough the fields, and scatter the good seed on the land,
But it is fed and watered by God's almighty hand:
He sends the snow in winter, the warmth to swell the grain,
The breezes and the sunshine, and soft, refreshing rain.
All good gifts around us are sent from heaven above;
Then thank the Lord, O thank the Lord, for all his love.

Matthias Claudius

Confession

There's a wideness in God's mercy
like the wideness of the sea.

F.W. FABER

L ord Jesus Christ,
  Son of God,
have mercy on me,
a sinner.

Eastern Orthodox prayer

Wilt thou forgive that sin where I begun,
Which was my sin, though it were done before?
Wilt thou forgive that sin through which I run,
And do run still, though still I do deplore?
When thou hast done, thou hast not done,
For I have more.

Wilt thou forgive that sin by which I have won
Others to sin, and made my sin their door?
Wilt thou forgive that sin which I did shun
A year or two, but wallowed in a score?
When thou hast done, thou hast not done,
For I have more.

I have a sin of fear, that when I have spun
My last thread, I shall perish on the shore;
But swear by thyself that at my death thy Son
Shall shine as he shines now and heretofore;
And, having done that, thou hast done,
I fear no more.

John Donne

Lord, have mercy upon us.
Christ, have mercy upon us.
Lord, have mercy upon us.

Oh Lord, hear our prayer.
And let our cry come unto thee.

The Book of Common Prayer

Have mercy on me, O God,
according to your unfailing love;
according to your great compassion
blot out my transgressions.
Wash away all my iniquity
and cleanse me from my sin.

For I know my transgressions,
and my sin is always before me.
Against you, you only, have I sinned
and done what is evil in your sight,
so that you are proved right when you speak
and justified when you judge.
Surely I was sinful at birth,
sinful from the time my mother conceived me.
Surely you desire truth in the inner parts;
you teach me wisdom in the inmost place.

Cleanse me with hyssop, and I shall be clean;
wash me, and I shall be whiter than snow.
Let me hear joy and gladness;
let the bones you have crushed rejoice.
Hide your face from my sins
and blot out all my iniquity.

Create in me a pure heart, O God,
and renew a steadfast spirit within me.
Do not cast me from your presence
or take your Holy Spirit from me.
Restore to me the joy of your salvation
and grant me a willing spirit, to sustain me.

Then I will teach transgressors your ways,
and sinners will turn back to you.
Save me from bloodguilt, O God,
the God who saves me,
and my tongue will sing of your righteousness.
O Lord, open my lips,
and my mouth will declare your praise.

You do not delight in sacrifice, or I would bring it;
you do not take pleasure in burnt offerings.
The sacrifices of God are a broken spirit;
a broken and contrite heart,
O God, you will not despise.

Psalm 51:1–17

Almighty and most merciful Father,
we have erred, and strayed from thy ways
like lost sheep.

We have followed too much the devices and desires
of our own hearts.
We have offended against thy holy laws.
We have left undone those things
which we ought to have done;
and we have done those things
which we ought not to have done;
and there is no health in us.
But thou, O Lord, have mercy upon us, miserable offenders.
Spare thou them, O God, that confess their faults.
Restore thou them that are penitent;
according to thy promises declared unto mankind
in Christ Jesu our Lord.
And grant, O merciful Father, for his sake;
that we may hereafter live a godly, righteous and sober life,
to the glory of thy holy name.

The Book of Common Prayer

O Lamb of God,
who takest away the sin of the world,
look upon us and have mercy upon us;
thou who art thyself both victim and priest,
thyself both reward and redeemer,
keep safe from all evil those whom thou hast redeemed,
O Saviour of the world.

St Irenaeus of Lyons

We beseech you, O Lord our God, be patient with us sinners.
You who know our weakness, protect the work of your hands
now and in times to come, deliver us from all temptation and all danger
and from the powers of darkness of this world,
and bring us into the kingdom of your only Son and our God.
For to your most holy name be the glory, Father, Son and Holy Spirit,
now and for ever, to the ages of ages. Amen.

Eastern Orthodox prayer

Out of the depths I cry to you, O Lord;
O Lord, hear my voice.
Let your ears be attentive
to my cry for mercy.

If you, O Lord, kept a record of sins,
O Lord, who could stand?
But with you there is forgiveness;
therefore you are feared.

I wait for the Lord, my soul waits,
and in his word I put my hope.
My soul waits for the Lord
more than watchmen wait for the morning,
more than watchmen wait for the morning.

O Israel, put your hope in the Lord,
for with the Lord is unfailing love
and with him is full redemption.
He himself will redeem Israel
from all their sins.

Psalm 130

Forgive them all, O Lord:
our sins of omission
and our sins of commission;
the sins of our youth
and the sins of our riper years;
the sins of our souls
and the sins of our bodies;
our secret and our more open sins;
our sins of ignorance and surprise,
and our more deliberate and presumptuous sins;
the sins we have done to please ourselves,
and the sins we have done to please others;
the sins we know and remember,
and the sins we have forgotten;
the sins we have striven to hide from others,
and the sins by which we have made others offend;
forgive them, O Lord, forgive them all for his sake,
who died for our sins and rose for our justification,
and now stands at thy right hand to make intercession for us,
Jesus Christ our Lord.

John Wesley

Almighty and everlasting God,
you hate nothing that you have made,
and forgive the sins of all those who are penitent.
Create and make in us new and contrite hearts
that lamenting our sins and acknowledging our wretchedness,
we may receive from you, the God of all mercy,
perfect forgiveness and peace,
through Jesus Christ our Lord. Amen.

Thomas Cranmer

Petition

Holy Father, in your mercy,
hear our earnest prayer.

Isabel Stevenson

We thank thee, Lord,
for the glory of the late days
and the excellent face of thy sun.
We thank thee for good news received.
We thank thee for the pleasures we have enjoyed
and for those we have been able to confer.
And now, when the clouds gather
and rain impends over the forest and our house,
permit us not to be cast down;
let us not lose the savour
of past mercies and past pleasures;
but, like the voice of a bird singing in the rain,
let grateful memory survive
in the hour of darkness.

Robert Louis Stevenson

As the rain hides the stars,
as the autumn mist hides the hills,
as the clouds veil the blue of the sky,
so the dark happenings of my lot
hide the shining of your face from me.
Yet, if I may hold your hand in the darkness,
it is enough, since I know that,
though I may stumble in my going,
you do not fall.

Celtic prayer, translated by Alistair MacLean

Teach us, Lord,
to serve you as you deserve,
to give and not to count the cost,
to fight and not to heed the wounds,
to toil and not to seek for rest,
to labour and not to seek for any reward
save that of knowing that we do your will.

St Ignatius Loyola

My God, my God, why have you forsaken me?
Why are you so far from saving me,
so far from the words of my groaning?
O my God, I cry out by day, but you do not answer,
by night, and am not silent.

Yet you brought me out of the womb;
you made me trust in you
even at my mother's breast.
From birth I was cast upon you;
from my mother's womb you have been my God.
Do not be far from me,
for trouble is near
and there is no one to help.

Psalm 22:1–2, 9–11

Calm my troubled heart;
give me peace.
O Lord, calm the waves of this heart,
calm its tempests!
Calm thyself, O my soul,
so that the divine can act in thee!
Calm thyself, O my soul,
so that God is able to repose in thee,
so that his peace may cover thee!
Yes, Father in heaven,
often have we found
that the world cannot give us peace,
but make us feel
that thou art able to give peace;
let us know the truth of thy promise:
that the whole world may not be able
to take away thy peace.

Søren Kierkegaard

L ord, I am tearing the heart of my soul in two.
I need you to come and lie there yourself
in the wounds of my soul.

Mechtild of Magdeburg

L ook, Father, look on his anointed face,
and only look on us as found in him;
look not on our misusings of thy grace,
our prayer so languid and our faith so dim.
For, lo, between our sins and their reward
we set the passion of thy Son our Lord.

William Bright

A lmighty God,
the fountain of all wisdom,
you know our needs before we ask,
and our ignorance in asking;
have compassion on our weakness,
and give us those things which for
our unworthiness we dare not,
and for our blindness we cannot ask,
for the sake of your Son, Jesus Christ our Lord.
Amen.

The Alternative Service Book

G ive us grace, O Lord,
not only to hear thy word with our ears,
but also to receive it into our hearts
and to show it forth in our lives;
for the glory of thy great name.

Anon

O my God,
stand by me
against all the world's wisdom and reason.
Not mine, but yours is the cause.
I would prefer to have peaceful days,
and to be out of this turmoil.
But yours, O Lord, is this cause;
it is righteous and eternal.
Stand by me, O God,
in the name of your dear Son, Jesus Christ,
who shall be my Defence and Shelter,
my Mighty Fortress,
through the might and strength of your Holy Spirit.
God help me.

Martin Luther

Write your blessed name,
O Lord,
upon my heart,
there to remain so indelibly engraved,
that no prosperity,
no adversity shall ever move me from your love.
Be to me a strong tower of defence,
a comforter in tribulation,
a deliverer in distress,
a very present help in trouble
and a guide to heaven
through the many temptations
and dangers of this life.

Thomas à Kempis

Behold, Lord,
an empty vessel that needs to be filled.
My Lord, fill it.
I am weak in the faith;
strengthen me.
I am cold in love;
warm me and make me fervent
that my love may go out to my neighbour.
I do not have a strong and firm faith;
at times I doubt
and am unable to trust you altogether.
O Lord, help me.
Strengthen my faith and trust in you.
In you I have sealed the treasures of all I have.
I am poor;
you are rich and came to be merciful to the poor.
I am a sinner; you are upright.
With me there is an abundance of sin;
in you is the fulness of righteousness.
Therefore I will remain with you
of whom I can receive
but to whom I may not give. Amen.

Martin Luther

Strengthen for service, Lord,
the hands that have taken holy things;
may the ears which have heard your word
be deaf to clamour and dispute;
may the tongues which have sung your praise
be free from deceit;
may the eyes which have seen the tokens of your love
shine with the light of hope;
and may the bodies which have been fed with your body
be refreshed with the fullness of your life;
glory to you for ever.

Syriac Liturgy of Malabar

Be thou my vision, O Lord of my heart;
Be all else but naught to me, save that thou art;
Be thou my best thought in the day and the night;
Both waking and sleeping, thy presence my light.

Be thou my wisdom, be thou my true word;
Be thou ever with me, and I with thee, Lord;
Be thou my great Father, and I thy true son;
Be thou in me dwelling, and I with thee one.

Be thou my breastplate, my sword for the fight;
Be thou my whole armour, be thou my true might;
Be thou my soul's shelter, be thou my strong tower;
O raise thou me heavenward, great Power of my power.

Riches I heed not, nor man's empty praise;
Be thou mine inheritance now and always;
Be thou and thou only the first in my heart;
O Sovereign of heaven, my treasure thou art.

High King of heaven, thou heaven's bright Sun;
O grant me its joys, after victory is won;
Great Heart of my own heart, whatever befall,
still be thou my vision, O Ruler of all.

Eighth-century prayer, translated Mary Byrne and Eleanor Hull

God be in my head
and in my understanding;
God be in my eyes
and in my looking;
God be in my mouth
and in my speaking;
God be in my heart
and in my thinking;
God be at my end
and at my departing.

The Book of Hours, sixteenth century

O my Lord,
  I am in a dry land,
all dried up and cracked
by the violence of the north wind and the cold;
but as you see,
I ask for nothing more;
you will send me
both dew and warmth
when it pleases you.

St Jane de Chantal

O God, the living God,
who has put your own eternity in our hearts,
and has made us to hunger and thirst after you:
satisfy, we pray you,
the instincts which you have implanted in us
that we may find you in life, and life in you;
through Jesus Christ our Lord.

Anon

Ah Lord, my prayers are dead,
my affections dead
and my heart is dead;
but you are a living God
and I bear myself upon you.

William Bridge

O Lord, I know not what to ask of thee.
Thou alone knowest what are my true needs.
Thou lovest me more than I myself know how to love.
Help me to see my real needs
which are concealed from me.
I dare not ask either a cross or consolation;
I can only wait on thee.
My heart is open to thee.
Visit and help me,
for thy great mercy's sake.
Strike me and heal me,
cast me down and raise me up.
I worship in silence thy holy will
and thine inscrutable ways.
I offer myself as a sacrifice to thee.
I put all my trust in thee.
I have no other desire than to fulfil thy will.
Teach me how to pray.
Pray thou thyself in me.

Metropolitan Philaret of Moscow

O ur Father in heaven,
hallowed be your name,
your kingdom come;
your will be done,
on earth as in heaven.
Give us today our daily bread.
Forgive us our sins
as we forgive those who sin against us.
Lead us not into temptation
but deliver us from evil.
For the kingdom, the power, and the glory are yours,
now and for ever. Amen.

The Lord's prayer

Intercession

We beg you, Lord,
to help and defend us.

St Clement of Rome

This is my song, O God of all nations,
a song of peace for lands afar, and mine.
This is my hope, the country where my heart is,
this is my hope, my dream and my shrine.
But other hearts in other lands are beating
with hopes and dreams that are the same as mine.
My country's skies are bluer than the ocean,
the sunlight beams on clover leafs and pine;
but other lands have sunlight too, and clover,
and other skies are just as blue as mine.
O hear my prayer, thou God of all the nations,
a prayer of peace for other lands and mine.

Anon

Pour forth,
O Christ,
your love
upon this land
today.

Anon

Almighty God,
as your Son our Saviour
was born of a Hebrew mother,
but rejoiced in the faith of a Syrian woman
and of a Roman soldier,
welcomed the Greeks who sought him,
and needed a man from Africa to carry his cross;
so teach us to regard the members of all races
as fellow heirs of the kingdom of Jesus Christ our Lord.

Prayer used by TOC H

Strengthen us, O God,
to relieve the oppressed,
to hear the groans of poor prisoners,
to reform the abuses of all professions;
that many be made not poor
to make a few rich;
for Jesus Christ's sake.

Oliver Cromwell

O God of peace,
good beyond all that is good,
in whom is calmness and concord,
heal the dissensions which divide us from one another,
and bring us into unity of love in you;
through Jesus Christ our Lord.

St Dionysius of Alexandria

O Lord,
we pray for the universal church,
for all sections of your church throughout the world,
for their truth, unity and stability,
that love may abound and truth flourish in them all.

We pray for our own church,
that what is lacking in it may be supplied
and what is unsound corrected;
and unto all men everywhere
give your grace and your blessing;
for the sake of Jesus Christ,
our only Lord and Saviour.

Lancelot Andrewes

O God, the father of the forsaken,
the help of the weak,
the supplier of the needy;
you teach us that love towards the race of man
is the bond of perfectness
and the imitation of your blessed self.

Open and touch our hearts
that we may see and do,
both for this world and that which is to come,
the things that belong to our peace.
Strengthen us in the work which we have undertaken;
give us wisdom, perseverance, faith and zeal,
and in your own time and according to your pleasure
prosper the issue;
for the love of your Son, Christ Jesus.

Lord Shaftesbury

Have mercy, O God, on all who are sorrowful,
those who weep and those in exile.
Have pity on the persecuted and the homeless
who are without hope;
those who are scattered in remote corners of this world;
those who are in prison and ruled by tyrants.
Have mercy on them as is written in your holy law,
where your compassion is exalted!

Jewish prayer

O God, graciously comfort and tend all who are imprisoned,
hungry, thirsty, naked and miserable;
also all widows, orphans, sick and sorrowing.
In brief, give us our daily bread,
so that Christ may abide in us and we in him for ever.

Martin Luther

H oly Father, in your mercy,
Hear our earnest prayer,
Keep our loved ones, now far distant,
'Neath your care.

When in sorrow, when in danger,
When in loneliness,
In your love look down and comfort
Their distress.

May the joy of your salvation
Be their strength and stay;
May they love and may they praise you
Day by day.

Isabel Stevenson

G rant, O Lord,
to all those who are bearing pain,
thy spirit of healing,
thy spirit of life,
thy spirit of peace and hope,
of courage and endurance.
Cast out from them
the spirit of anxiety and fear;
grant them perfect confidence
and trust in thee,
that in thy light they may see light,
through Jesus Christ our Lord.

Anon

Lord Christ, you see us
    sometimes like strangers on the earth,
taken aback by the violence,
by the harshness of oppositions.
And you come to send out a gentle breeze
on the dry ground of our doubts,
and so prepare us to be bearers
of peace and of reconciliation.

Brother Roger of Taizé

We beg you, Lord,
to help and defend us.
Deliver the oppressed,
pity the insignificant, raise the fallen,
show yourself to the needy, heal the sick,
bring back those of your people
who have gone astray,
feed the hungry, lift up the weak,
take off the prisoners' chains.
May every nation come to know
that you alone are God,
that Jesus Christ is your child,
that we are your people,
the sheep of your pasture.

St Clement of Rome

Lord Jesus Christ, who will, in the end,
acknowledge all acts of mercy as done to you,
grant that we may never pass by the poor,
but may respond with generous hearts
to the voice of the helpless, whose cry is your own.

Anon

Christ has no body now on earth but yours,
no hands but yours,
no feet but yours;
yours are the eyes
through which he looks with compassion on the world,
yours are the feet
with which he is to go about doing good,
and yours are the hands
with which he is to bless us now.

St Teresa of Avila

Morning and Evening

Christ with me watching,
every day and night.

CARMINA GADELICA

O God of love,
true light and radiance of our world,
shine into our hearts like the rising sun,
and banish the darkness of sin and the mists of error.
May we, this day and all our life,
walk without stumbling
along the way which you have set before us;
through your Son Jesus Christ our Lord.

Desiderius Erasmus

Come into my soul, Lord,
as the dawn breaks into the sky;
let your sun rise in my heart
at the coming of the day.

Anon

O Lord, the day is yours, and the night is yours;
you have prepared the light and the sun;
they continue this day according to your ordinance,
for all things serve you.
Blessed are you, O Lord,
for you turn the shadow of death into the morning,
and renew the face of the earth.

Lancelot Andrewes

This is the day the Lord has made;
let us rejoice and be glad in it.

Psalm 118:24

O Lord,
grant me to greet the coming day in peace.
Help me in all things to rely upon your holy will.
In every hour of the day reveal your will to me.
Bless my dealings with all who surround me.
Teach me to treat all that comes to me throughout the day
with peace of soul and with firm conviction
that your will governs all.
In all my deeds and words guide my thoughts and feelings.
In unforeseen events let me not forget that all are sent by you.
Teach me to act firmly and wisely
without embittering or embarrassing others.
Give me strength to bear the fatigue of the coming day
with all that it shall bring.
Direct my will, teach me to pray, pray yourself in me.

Metropolitan Philaret of Moscow

O you most holy and ever-loving God,
we thank you once more
for the quiet rest of the night that has gone by,
for the new promise that has come with this fresh morning,
and for the hope of this day.
While we have slept,
the world in which we live has swept on,
and we have rested under the shadow of your love.
May we trust you this day
for all the needs of the body, the soul, and the spirit.
Give us this day our daily bread. Amen.

Robert Collyer

My Father, for another night
Of quiet sleep and rest,
For all the joy of morning light,
Your holy name be blest.

Henry William Baker

O Christ, our Morning Star,
Splendour of Light Eternal,
shining with the glory of the rainbow,
come and waken us
from the greyness of our apathy
and renew in us your gift of hope.

The Venerable Bede

I rise today
with the power of God to guide me,
the might of God to uphold me,
the wisdom of God to teach me,
the eye of God to watch over me,
the ear of God to hear me,
the word of God to give me speech,
the hand of God to protect me,
the path of God to lie before me,
the shield of God to shelter me,
the host of God to defend me
against the snares of the devil
and the temptations of the world,
against every man who meditates
injury against me, whether far or near.

St Patrick of Ireland

O secret Christ,
Lord of the rose of dawn,
hide me within thy silent peace,
that throughout the turmoil of the day,
I may abide within the quiet of the daybreak.

Anon

Day is done,
Gone the sun
From the lake, from the hills, from the sky.
Safely rest,
All is well!
God is nigh.

Anon

Lighten our darkness,
Lord, we pray;
and in your mercy defend us
from all perils and dangers of this night;
for the love of your only Son,
our Saviour Jesus Christ.

The Alternative Service Book

While I sleep, O Lord,
let my heart not cease to worship you;
fill my sleep with your presence,
while creation itself keeps watch,
singing psalms with the angels,
and taking up my soul into its paean of praise.

St Gregory of Nazianzus

Be with us, merciful God,
and protect us through the silent hours of this night;
that we, who are wearied by the changes and chances
of this fleeting world,
may rest upon your eternal changelessness;
through Jesus Christ our Lord. Amen.

The Office of Compline

The day thou gavest, Lord, is ended,
The darkness falls at thy behest;
To thee our morning hymns ascended,
Thy praise shall sanctify our rest.

We thank thee that thy Church unsleeping
While earth rolls onward into light,
Through all the world her watch is keeping,
And rests not now by day or night.

As o'er each continent and island
The dawn leads on another day,
The voice of prayer is never silent,
Nor dies the strain of praise away.

The sun that bids us rest is waking
Our brethren 'neath the western sky,
And hour by hour fresh lips are making
Thy wondrous doings heard on high.

So be it, Lord; thy throne shall never,
Like earth's proud empires, pass away;
Thy kingdom stands, and grows for ever,
Till all thy creatures own thy sway.

John Ellerton

Abide with me;
Fast falls the eventide;
The darkness deepens;
Lord, with me abide;
When other helpers fail,
And other comforts flee,
Help of the helpless,
O abide with me.

Henry Francis Lyte

Answer me when I call to you,
O my righteous God.
Give me relief from my distress;
be merciful to me and hear my prayer.

Many are asking,
'Who can show us any good?'
Let the light of your face shine upon us, O Lord.
You have filled my heart with greater joy
than when their grain and new wine abound.
I will lie down and sleep in peace,
for you alone, O Lord,
make me dwell in safety.

Psalm 4:1, 6–8

Watch, dear Lord,
with those who wake or weep tonight,
and let your angels protect those who sleep.
Tend the sick.
Refresh the weary.
Sustain the dying.
Calm the suffering.
Pity the distressed.
We ask this for your love's sake.

St Augustine of Hippo

Alone with none but thee, my God,
I journey on my way.
What need I fear, when thou art near,
O king of night and day?
More safe am I within thy hand
Than if a host did round me stand.

St Columba of Iona

Blessed are you,
O Lord our God,
King of the universe!
At your word night falls.
In your wisdom
you open heaven's gates,
you control the elements
and rotate the seasons.
You set the stars
in the vault of heaven.
You created night and day.
You cause the light to fade
when darkness comes
and the darkness to melt away
in the light of the new day.
O ever-living and eternal God,
you will always watch over us,
your creatures.
Blessed are you, O Lord,
at whose word night falls.

Jewish prayer

God with me lying down,
God with me rising up,
God with me in each ray of light,
nor I a ray of joy without him,
nor one ray without him.

Christ with me sleeping,
Christ with me waking,
Christ with me watching,
every day and night,
each day and night.

God with me protecting,
the Lord with me directing,
the Spirit with me strengthening,
for ever and for evermore,
ever and evermore, amen.
chief of chiefs, amen.

Carmina Gadelica

Lord, you have always given
bread for the coming day;
and though I am poor,
today I believe.

Lord, you have always given
strength for the coming day;
and though I am weak,
today I believe.

Lord, you have always given
peace for the coming day;
and though of anxious heart,
today I believe.

Lord, you have always kept
me safe in trials;
and now, tried as I am,
today I believe.

Lord, you have always marked
the road for the coming day;
and though it may be hidden,
today I believe.

Lord, you have always lightened
this darkness of mine;
and though the night is here,
today I believe.

Lord, you have always spoken
when time was ripe;
and though you be silent now,
today I believe.

Used by the Northumbria Community

The Church Year

Christ has died,
Christ is risen,
Christ will come again.

THE BOOK OF COMMON PRAYER

ADVENT

A^{t Advent}
we should try the key to our heart's door.
It may have gathered rust.
If so, this is the time to oil it,
in order that the heart's door may open
more easily when the Lord Jesus
wants to enter at Christmas time!

Lord, oil the hinges of our hearts' doors
that they may swing gently and easily
to welcome your coming.

New Guinea prayer

Eternal Light,
shine into our hearts,
eternal Goodness,
deliver us from evil,
eternal Power,
be our support,
eternal Wisdom,
scatter the darkness of our ignorance,
eternal Pity,
have mercy upon us,
that with all our heart and mind
and soul and strength
we may seek your face
and be brought by your infinite mercy
to your holy presence;
through Jesus Christ our Lord.

Alcuin of York

Father in heaven,
our hearts desire the warmth of your love
and our minds are searching
for the light of your word.

Increase our longing for Christ our Saviour
and give us the strength to grow in love,
that the dawn of his coming
may find us rejoicing in his presence
and welcoming the light of his truth.

The Roman Missal

CHRISTMAS

Hail King! hail King! blessed is he! blessed is he!
Hail King! hail King! blessed is he! blessed is he!
Hail King! hail King! blessed is he!
The King of whom we sing,
All hail! let there be joy!

This night is the eve of the great nativity,
Born is the Son of Mary the Virgin,
The soles of his feet have reached the earth,
The Son of glory down from on high,
Heaven and earth glowed to him,
All Hail! let there be joy!

The peace of earth to him, the joy of heaven to him,
Behold his feet have reached the world;
The homage of a King be his, the welcome of a Lamb be his,
King all victorious, Lamb all glorious,
Earth and ocean illumed to him,
All hail! let there be joy!

The mountains glowed to him, the plains glowed to him,
The voice of the waves with the song of the strand,
Announcing to us that Christ is born,
Son of the King of kings from the land of salvation;
Shone the sun on the mountains high to him,
All hail! let there be joy!

Shone to him the earth and sphere together,
God the Lord has opened a Door;
Son of Mary Virgin, hasten thou to help me,
Thou Christ of hope, Thou Door of joy,
Golden Sun of hill and mountain,
All hail! let there be joy!

Offer to the Being from found to cover,
Include stave and stone and beam;
Offer again both rods and cloth,
Be health to the people therein,
Hail King! hail King! blessed is he! blessed is he!
Hail King! hail King! blessed is he! blessed is he!
Ho, hail! blessed the King!
Let there be joy!

Blessed the King,
Without beginning, without ending,
To everlasting, to eternity,
Every generation for aye,
Ho! hi! let there be joy!

Scottish prayer

L oving Father,
   help us remember the birth of Jesus,
that we may share in the song of the angels,
the gladness of the shepherds
and the wisdom of the wise men.

Close the door of hate
and open the door of love all over the world.

Let kindness come with every gift
and good desires with every greeting.

Deliver us from evil by the blessing which Christ brings
and teach us to be merry with clean hearts.

May the Christmas morning
make us happy to be your children
and the Christmas evening
bring us to our beds with grateful thoughts,
forgiving and forgiven, for Jesus' sake. Amen.

Robert Louis Stevenson

Hark! the herald-angels sing
Glory to the newborn King,
Peace on earth and mercy mild,
God and sinners reconciled.
Joyful, all ye nations rise,
Join the triumph of the skies;
With the angelic host proclaim,
'Christ is born in Bethlehem.'
Hark! the herald-angels sing
Glory to the newborn King.

Charles Wesley

We pray you, Lord,
to purify our hearts
that they may be worthy
to become your dwelling place.
Let us never fail to find room for you,
but come and abide in us,
that we also may abide in you,
for at this time
you were born into the world for us,
and live and reign,
King of kings and Lord of lords,
now and for ever.

William Temple

And now we give you thanks
because in his coming as man
the day of our deliverance has dawned;
and through him you will make all things new,
as he comes in power and triumph to judge the world.

The Alternative Service Book

Almighty God,
give us grace to cast away the works of darkness
and to put on the armour of light,
now in the time of this mortal life,
in which your Son Jesus Christ came to us
in great humility;
so that on the last day,
when he shall come again in his glorious majesty
to judge the living and the dead,
we may rise to the life immortal,
through him who is alive and reigns with you
and the Holy Spirit, now and ever. Amen.

The Alternative Service Book

The child of glory,
the child of Mary,
born in the stable
the king of all,
who came to the wilderness
and in our stead suffered;
happy they are counted
who to him are near.

Celtic prayer

Almighty God,
you make us glad with the yearly remembrance
of the birth of your Son Jesus Christ.
Grant that as we joyfully receive him for our redeemer,
we may with sure confidence behold him
when he shall come to be our judge;
who is alive and reigns with you and the Holy Spirit
one God, now and for ever.

The Alternative Service Book

Lent

We thank you, Father,
for those days in the desert when,
through prayer and fasting,
Jesus discovered your will for his life
and overcame the temptations of the Evil One.

Help us,
during these days of Lent,
to come close to you
and to listen to your voice.
Give us strength
to overcome the temptation
to please ourselves
and live life without you.
Teach us your way. For Jesus' sake.

The Alternative Service Book

Who goeth in the way which Christ hath gone,
Is much more sure to meet with him than one
That travelleth byways:
Perhaps my God, though he be far before,
May turn, and take me by the hand, and more
May strengthen my decays.

Yet, Lord, instruct us to improve our fast
By starving sin and taking such repast
As may our faults control:
That every man may revel at his door,
Not in his parlour; banqueting the poor,
And among those his soul.

George Herbert

EASTER

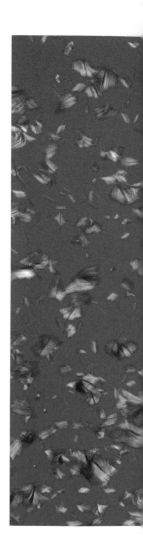

L ord, who createdst man in wealth and store,
       Though foolishly he lost the same,
Decaying more and more,
Till he became
Most poor:
With thee
O let me rise,
As larks, harmoniously,
And sing this day thy victories:
Then shall the fall further the flight in me.

My tender age in sorrow did begin:
And still with sicknesses and shame
Thou didst so punish sin,
That I became
Most thin.
With thee
Let me combine,
And feel this day thy victory:
For, if I imp my wing on thine,
Affliction shall advance the flight in me.

George Herbert

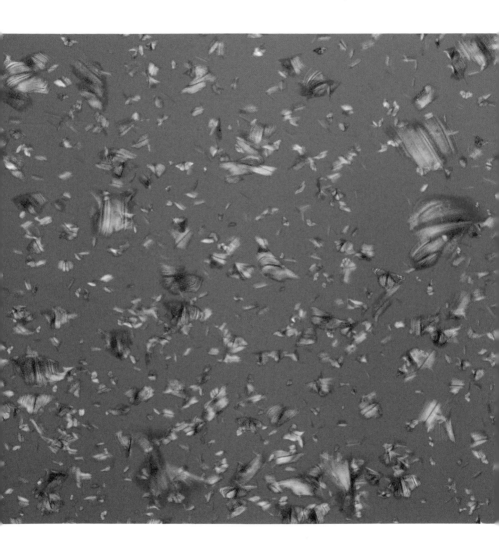

Christ has risen from the dead,
by death defeating death,
and those buried in the grave
he has brought back to life.

Orthodox prayer

This is that night of tears, the three days' space,
Sorrow abiding of the eventide,
Until the day break with the risen Christ,
And hearts that sorrowed shall be satisfied.

So may our hearts have pity on thee, Lord,
That they may sharers of thy glory be:
Heavy with weeping may the three days pass,
To win the laughter of thine Easter Day.

Peter Abelard

Not because of your promised heaven
Do I wish to devote my love to you;
Nor from dread of a much-feared hell
Do I wish to cease from offending you.
You touch me, Lord, when I see you nailed –
Nailed on a cross – when I see you mocked;
I am stirred by the sight of your body bruised,
By your sufferings too and by your death.
I am stirred by your love in such a way
That even without hope of heaven I shall love you
And without any fear of hell I shall fear you.
Naught you need give me that I may love you,
For even without hoping for the hope that is mine
I shall love you as love you I do.

Attributed to St Francis Xavier

The strife is o'er, the battle is done;
Now is the victor's triumph won,
O let the song of praise be sung:
Alleluia!

Eighth-century prayer

If you were not risen,
Lord Christ, to whom would we go
to discover a radiance
of the face of God?

If you were not risen,
we would not be together
seeking your communion.
We would not find in your presence forgiveness,
wellspring of a new beginning.

If you were not risen,
where would we draw the energy
for following you
right to the end of our existence,
for choosing you again and anew?

Brother Roger of Taizé

Lord, teach us to understand
that your Son died to save us
not from suffering but from ourselves,
not from injustice, far less from justice,
but from being unjust.
He died that we might live –
but live as he lives, by dying as he died
who died to himself.

George Macdonald

Lord Jesus Christ,
who prayed for your disciples
that they might be one,
even as you are one with the Father,
draw us to yourself,
that in common love and obedience to you
we may be united to one another,
that the world may believe that you are Lord,
to the glory of God the Father.

William Temple

Then let us feast this Easter Day
On Christ, the bread of heaven.
The Word of grace has purged away
The old and evil leaven.
Christ alone our souls will feed;
He is our meat and drink indeed;
Faith lives upon no other!
Alleluia!

Martin Luther

When I survey the wondrous cross
On which the Prince of Glory died,
My richest gain I count but loss,
And pour contempt on all my pride.

Forbid it, Lord, that I should boast,
Save in the death of Christ my God;
All the vain things that charm me most,
I sacrifice them to his blood.

See, from his head, his hands, his feet,
Sorrow and love flow mingled down;
Did e'er such love and sorrow meet,
Or thorns compose so rich a crown?

Were the whole realm of nature mine,
That were an offering far too small;
Love so amazing, so divine,
Demands my soul, my life, my all.

Isaac Watts

ASCENSION

Lord Jesus, we remember
how you returned to your Father
on the first Ascension Day.
Although we cannot see you with our eyes,
we know that you are still with us
as you promised always to be.
We thank you for being our constant friend.
Help us to remember that you are near
and that you will never fail us.
Help us to come to you
when we are frightened or disappointed,
and may we remember to tell you
about our joys as well as our troubles.

O Lord Jesus Christ,
who after your resurrection from the dead
did gloriously ascend into heaven,
grant us the aid of your loving-kindness,
that according to your promise
you may ever dwell with us on earth,
and we with you in heaven,
where with the Father and the Holy Ghost,
you live and reign one God for ever and ever.
Amen.

The Gelasian Sacramentary

Christ has died,
Christ is risen,
Christ will come again.

The Book of Common Prayer

PENTECOST

O God,
you have graciously brought us to this hour,
the time when you poured out your Holy Spirit
in tongues of fire upon your apostles,
filling them with the gift of your grace;
so, most wonderful Lord,
may we too receive this blessing;
and as we seek to praise you, merciful God,
in psalms and hymns and spiritual songs,
may we share in your eternal kingdom.
For your name is worthy of all honour and majesty
and you are to be glorified in hymns of blessing,
Father, Son and Holy Spirit,
now and for ever, to the ages of ages. Amen.

Eastern Orthodox Church

Spirit of God, with your holy breath
you cleanse the hearts and minds of your people;
you comfort them when they are in sorrow,
you lead them when they wander from the way,
you kindle them when they are cold,
you knit them together when they are at variance,
and you enrich them with many and various gifts.
We beseech you daily to increase
those gifts which you have entrusted to us;
that with your light before us and within us
we may pass through this world
without stumbling and without straying.

Desiderius Erasmus

Holy Spirit:
As the wind is your symbol, so forward our goings.
As the dove, so launch us heavenwards.
As water, so purify our spirits.
As a cloud, so abate our temptations.
As dew, so revive our languor.
As fire, so purge out our dross.

Christina Rossetti

Through the Holy Spirit
we are restored to paradise,
led back to the kingdom of heaven,
and adopted as children,
given confidence to call God 'Father'
and to share in Christ's grace,
called children of light
and given a share in eternal glory.

St Basil the Great

Come down, O Love divine,
Seek thou this soul of mine,
And visit it with thine own ardour glowing;
O Comforter, draw near,
Within my heart appear,
And kindle it, thy holy flame bestowing.

O let it freely burn,
Till earthly passions turn
To dust and ashes, in its heat consuming;
And let thy glorious light
Shine ever on my sight,
And clothe me round, the while my path illuming.

Bianco da Siena

Breathe in me, Holy Spirit,
that I may think what is holy.

Move me, Holy Spirit,
that I may do what is holy.

Attract me, Holy Spirit,
that I may love what is holy.

Strengthen me, Holy Spirit,
that I may guard what is holy.

Guard me, Holy Spirit,
that I may keep what is holy.

St Augustine of Hippo

Come, Holy Spirit,
fill the hearts of thy faithful
and kindle in them the fire of thy love.

Let us pray, O God,
who didst instruct the hearts of the faithful
by the light of the Holy Spirit,
grant us in the same Spirit to be truly wise,
and ever to rejoice in his consolation.
Through Christ our Lord.
Amen.

The Roman Missal

Church Rites

Open our hearts and minds,
so that we may be renewed
by your power.

ANON

BAPTISM

Creator Spirit,
who in the beginning
hovered over the waters,
who at Jesus' baptism
descended in the form of a dove,
and who at Pentecost
was poured out
under the signs of fire and wind:
come to us,
open our hearts and minds,
so that we may hear
the life-giving word
and be renewed
by your power,
in the unity of the Father
and the Son,
now and for ever.
Amen.

Anon

May your feet walk
in the way of the Lord;
may your voice speak
the word of God;
may your hands serve God
in blessing others;
may your life show
something of the glory of God;
may you know the peace of God
now and always.

Anon

He has rescued us
from the dominion of darkness
and brought us into the kingdom
of the Son he loves.

Colossians 1:13

Almighty God, who by our baptism
into the death and resurrection
of thy Son Jesus Christ
dost turn us from the old life of sin:
grant that we, being reborn to new life in him,
may live in righteousness and holiness all our days;
through the same thy Son Jesus Christ our Lord,
who liveth and reigneth with thee and the Holy Spirit,
one God, now and for ever. Amen.

The Book of Common Prayer

O Lord our God,
look mercifully on us
and on those who are preparing
for Holy Baptism,
and have their heads bowed before you now:
make the light of your Gospel
shine upon them;
send an angel of light
to deliver them from all powers of the enemy,
that when they are fit to receive your immortal gift
and are brought into a life
of obedience to your commandments,
they may know the joys of heaven.
For you are their light
and we glorify you,
Father, Son and Holy Spirit,
now and for ever,
to the ages of ages. Amen.

Orthodox prayer

Therefore, if anyone is in Christ,
he is a new creation;
the old has gone,
the new has come!

2 Corinthians 5:17

MARRIAGE

O gracious and ever-living God,
you have created us to be the bearers of your love.
Look mercifully upon these two persons
who come seeking your blessing
and assist them with your grace,
that with fidelity and lasting love
they may honour and keep the vows and promises
which they make;
through Jesus Christ our Saviour, we pray. Amen.

The Book of Common Prayer

T he Lord sanctify and bless you,
the Lord pour the riches of his grace upon you,
that you may please him
and live together in holy love to your lives' end.
So be it.

John Knox

E ternal God,
true and loving Father,
in holy marriage you make your servants one.
May their life together
witness to your love in this troubled world;
may unity overcome division,
forgiveness heal injury,
and joy triumph over sorrow;
through Jesus Christ our Lord. Amen.

The Alternative Service Book

CONFIRMATION

Grant us, Lord,
to continue as we have begun,
with faith, prayer
and the strength of your Holy Spirit.
Through good and bad times,
through joy and sorrow,
through success and setbacks,
help us to hold fast
to the faith we have professed,
knowing that you,
who have called us,
are faithful, trustworthy and true.

Rebecca Winter

Just as I am, without one plea,
But that thy blood wast shed for me,
And that thou bidst me come to thee,
O Lamb of God, I come.

Charlotte Elliott

Defend, O Lord,
this thy child with thy heavenly grace,
that he may continue thine for ever;
and daily increase in the Holy Spirit,
more and more,
until he come unto thy everlasting kingdom.

Order of Confirmation, 1552

COMMUNION

Most gracious Father,
who callest us to the Holy Table of our Saviour,
to show his death and to receive his gift of life,
enable us to come with earnest faith and kindled devotion.
Help us to make the memorial of our Saviour's sacrifice
with adoration and praise.
Open our eyes to behold the vision of his love,
and pour into our souls the fulness of his grace.
And grant that yielding ourselves to thee,
we may henceforth live as those who are not their own,
but are bought with a price;
through Jesus Christ our Lord,
to whom with thee and the Holy Spirit
be all honour and glory, world without end.

The Church of Scotland: Book of Common Order

Almighty God,
we thank you for feeding us
with the body and blood of your Son, Jesus Christ.
Through him we offer you our souls and bodies
to be a living sacrifice.
Send us out in the power of your Spirit
to live and work
to your praise and glory.

The Alternative Service Book

O Lord, thank you for bread,
    your body, given for me;
thank you for wine,
your blood, poured out for me.
May this spiritual food be my strength and my joy,
until I come to you again.

Anon

For the bread and for the wine,
For the pledge that seals him mine,
For the words of love divine,
We give thee thanks, O Lord.

For the body and the blood,
For the more than angel's food,
For the boundless grace of God,
We give thee thanks, O Lord.

For the chalice whence we sip
Moisture for the parched lip,
For the board of fellowship,
We give thee thanks, O Lord.

For the feast of love and peace
Bidding all our sorrows cease,
Earnest of the kingdom's bliss,
We give thee thanks, O Lord.

For the paschal lamb here given,
For the loaf without the leaven,
For the manna dropped from heaven,
We give thee thanks, O Lord.

Only bread and only wine,
Yet to faith the solemn sign
Of the heavenly and divine!
We give thee thanks, O Lord.

Horatius Bonar

FUNERALS

Bring us, O Lord our God,
at our last awakening
into the house and gate of heaven,
to enter into that gate and dwell in that house,
where there shall be no darkness or dazzling,
but one equal light;
no noise or silence,
but one equal music;
no fears or hopes,
but one equal possession;
no ends or beginnings,
but one equal eternity;
in the habitations of thy glory and dominion
world without end.

John Donne

We give back to you, O God,
those whom you gave to us.
You did not lose them when you gave them to us,
and we do not lose them by their return to you.
Your Son has taught us
that life is eternal and love cannot die.
So death is only a horizon,
and a horizon is only the limit of our sight.
Open our eyes to see more clearly,
and draw us closer to you,
so that we may know we are nearer to our loved ones,
who are with you.
You have told us
that you are preparing a place for us:
prepare us, that where you are we may be always,
O dear Lord of life and death.

William Penn

Give rest, O Christ,
to your servant with your saints:
where sorrow and pain are no more;
neither sighing, but life everlasting.

You alone are immortal,
the creator and maker of man;
and we are mortal,
formed from the earth,
and to the earth we shall return;
for you so ordained when you created us, saying,
'Dust you are, and to dust you shall return;'
we shall all go down to the dust;
and, weeping over the grave, we sing
alleluia, alleluia, alleluia.

Give rest, O Christ,
to your servant with your saints:
where sorrow and pain are no more;
neither sighing, but life everlasting.

Russian Liturgy, sixth century

Into your hands, O Lord and Father,
we commend our souls and our bodies,
our parents and our homes,
friends and servants,
neighbours and kindred,
our benefactors and departed brethren,
all your people faithfully believing
and all who need your pity and protection.
Enlighten us with your holy grace
and suffer us never more to be separated from you,
one God in Trinity, God everlasting.

Edmund of Abingdon

Graces and Blessings

Deep peace of Christ,
the Son of Peace, to you.

SCOTTISH CELTIC PRAYER

Blessed are you,
Lord God of all creation.
Generously you give us the fruits of the earth
to delight and nourish us.
Bless this meal
and strengthen us in your service;
through Christ our Lord.

Anon

May all who share these gifts today
Be blessed by thee, we humbly pray.
What God gives and what we take
'Tis a gift for Christ his sake;
Be the meal of beans or peas,
God be thanked for those and these;
Have we flesh or have we fish,
All are fragments from his dish.

Robert Herrick

Bless, O Lord,
the plants, the vegetation,
and the herbs of the field,
that they may grow and increase to fullness
and bear much fruit.
And may the fruit of the land
remind us of the spiritual fruit we should bear.

Egyptian Coptic Orthodox liturgy

To God who gives our daily bread
A thankful song we raise,
And pray that he who sends our food
May fill our hearts with praise.

Thomas Tallis

You who give food to all flesh,
who feeds the young ravens that cry unto you
and has nourished us from our youth up:
fill our hearts with good and gladness
and establish our hearts with your grace.

Lancelot Andrewes

Bless, O Lord, this food to our use
and ourselves to your service,
and make us mindful of the needs of others;
for your love's sake.

Anon

Be present at our table, Lord,
be here and everywhere adored:
thy creatures bless, and grant that we
may feast in paradise with thee.

John Cennick

God bless the house
from site to stay,
from beam to wall,
from end to end,
from ridge to basement,
from balk to roof-tree,
from found to summit,
found and summit.

Celtic prayer

Do thou, O God, bless unto me
each thing mine eye doth see;
do thou, O God, bless unto me
each sound that comes to me;
do thou, O God, bless unto me
each taste in mouth doth dwell;
each sound that goes unto my song,
each ray that guides my way,
each thing that I pursue along,
each lure that tempts to stray,
the zeal that seeks my living soul,
the Three that seek my heart and whole,
the zeal that seeks my living soul,
the Three that seek my heart and whole.

Scottish prayer

The Lord bless you and keep you;
the Lord make his face shine upon you
and be gracious to you;
the Lord turn his face towards you
and give you peace.

Numbers 6:24–26

May the road rise up to meet you,
may the wind be always at your back,
may the sun shine upon your face,
the rains fall soft upon your fields
and, until we meet again,
may God hold you in the palm of his hand.

Irish prayer

May the everlasting Father himself take you
in his own generous clasp,
in his own generous arm.
May the everlasting Father shield you
east and west wherever you go.

Carmina Gadelica

Deep peace of the running waves to you,
deep peace of the flowing air to you,
deep peace of the quiet earth to you,
deep peace of the shining stars to you,
deep peace of the shades of night to you,
moon and stars always giving light to you,
deep peace of Christ, the Son of Peace, to you.

Scots Celtic prayer

The peace of God,
which passeth all understanding,
keep your hearts and minds
in the knowledge and love of God,
and of his Son, Jesus Christ our Lord:
and the blessing of God Almighty,
the Father, the Son, and the Holy Ghost,
be amongst you and remain with you always.

Holy Communion, 1549

May the grace of the Lord Jesus Christ,
and the love of God,
and the fellowship of the Holy Spirit
be with us all, evermore. Amen.

Based on 2 Corinthians 13:14

INDEX OF AUTHORS

Peter Abelard 94
Alcuin of York 85
Lancelot Andrewes 34, 66, 73, 118
Henry William Baker 74
John Kendrick Bangs 42
The Venerable Bede 75
Boethius 17
Horatius Bonar 111
William Bridge 61
William Bright 55
John Cennick 118
John Chapman 40
Matthias Claudius 42
Robert Collyer 74
Thomas Cranmer 50
Oliver Cromwell 66
John Donne 45, 112
Edmund of Abingdon 114
John Ellerton 78
Charlotte Elliott 108
Desiderius Erasmus 18, 72, 99
F.W. Faber 43
Charles de Foucauld 19
Père Grou 20
George Herbert 6, 23, 29, 38, 91, 92
Robert Herrick 117
Gilbert of Hoyland 32
Father John of the Russian Church 39
J.H. Jowett 41
Julian of Norwich 15
Thomas à Kempis 57
Thomas Ken 31
Søren Kierkegaard 54
John Knox 107
Martin Luther 56, 58, 67, 96
Henry Francis Lyte 78
George Macdonald 95
Mechtild of Magdeburg 55

John Milton 30
William Penn 113
Metropolitan Philaret of Moscow 62, 74
Hsieh Ping-hsin 20
Sir Walter Raleigh 31
Walter Rauschenbusch 36
Martin Rinckart 34
Brother Roger of Taizé 17, 69, 95
Christina Rossetti 100
Utsonomya San 20
Lord Shaftesbury 67
William Shakespeare 35
Bianco da Siena 100
St Ambrose of Milan 11, 18
St Augustine of Hippo 15, 79, 102
St Basil the Great 100
St Benedict of Nursia 14
St Catherine of Siena 12
St Clement of Rome 63, 70
St Columba of Iona 16, 79
St Dionysius of Alexandria 66
St Francis of Assisi 3, 22, 27, 29
St Francis Xavier 94
St Gregory of Nazianzus 76
St Ignatius Loyola 19, 52
St Irenaeus of Lyons 47
St Jane de Chantal 60
St Patrick of Ireland 18, 75
St Richard of Chichester 39
St Teresa of Avila 70
St Thérèse of Lisieux 20
Isabel Stevenson 51, 68
Robert Louis Stevenson 52, 87
Thomas Tallis 117
William Temple 88, 95
Isaac Watts 97
Charles Wesley 88
John Wesley 50
Rebecca Winter 108

Abide with me   78
Agreeing to lose everything for you, O Christ   17
Ah Lord, my prayers are dead   61
All is silent   20
Almighty and everlasting God   50
Almighty and most merciful Father   47
Almighty God, as your Son our Saviour   65
Almighty God, give us grace to cast away the works of darkness   90
Almighty God, the fountain of all wisdom   55
Almighty God, we thank you for feeding us   110
Almighty God, who by our baptism   106
Almighty God, you make us glad with the yearly remembrance   90
Alone with none but thee, my God   79
And now we give you thanks   89
Answer me when I call to you   79
As the deer longs for flowing streams   12
As the hand is made for holding   22
As the rain hides the stars   52
At Advent   84

Be present at our table, Lord   118
Be thou my vision, O Lord of my heart   59
Be with us, merciful God   77
Behold, Lord, an empty vessel that needs to be filled   58
Bless, O Lord   117
Bless, O Lord, this food to our use   118
Blessed are you, Lord God of all creation   116
Blessed are you, O Lord our God   80
Breathe in me, Holy Spirit   102
Bring us, O Lord our God   112

Calm my troubled heart   54
Christ has died   83, 98
Christ has no body now on earth but yours   70
Christ has risen from the dead   93
Christ with me watching   71
Come down, O Love divine   100
Come into my soul, Lord   72
Come, Holy Spirit   102
Creator Spirit   104

Day is done   76

Deep peace of Christ   115
Deep peace of the running waves to you   121
Defend, O Lord   109
Do thou, O God, bless unto me   119

Eternal God, true and loving Father   107
Eternal Light, shine into our hearts   85
Eternal Trinity, you are a deep sea   12

Father in heaven, our hearts desire the warmth of your love   85
For summer rains, and winter's sun   42
For the bread and for the wine   111
Forgive them all, O Lord   50

Give rest, O Christ   114
Give thanks to the Lord, for he is good   39
Give us grace, O Lord   55
Glorious Lord, I give you greeting!   26
Glory to the Father   31
God be in my head   59
God bless the house   118
God with me lying down   81
God, of your goodness   15
Grant us, Lord   108
Grant, O Lord, to all those who are bearing pain   68

Hail King! hail King! blessed is he! blessed is he!   86
Hark! the herald-angels sing   88
Have mercy on me, O God   46
Have mercy, O God, on all who are sorrowful   67
He has rescued us   105
Holy Father, in your mercy   51
Holy Father, in your mercy   68
Holy Spirit: As the wind is your symbol, so forward our goings   100

I am giving thee worship   30
I believe, O Lord and God of the peoples   25
I bind unto myself today   18
I rise today   75
I thank you, O God   37
If my lips could sing as many songs   25
If you were not risen   95
Into your hands, O Lord and Father   114

Just as I am, without one plea   108

Let all the world in every corner sing   23, 29
Let us, with a gladsome mind   30
Lighten our darkness   76
Look, Father, look on his anointed face   55
Lord Christ, you see us   69
Lord Jesus Christ, Son of God   44
Lord Jesus Christ, who prayed for your disciples   95
Lord Jesus Christ, who will in the end   70
Lord Jesus Christ, you said that you are   18
Lord Jesus, I am not an eagle   20
Lord Jesus, I give thee my hands to do thy work   34
Lord Jesus, we remember   98
Lord, have mercy upon us   45
Lord, I am tearing the heart of my soul in two   55
Lord, take as your right   19
Lord, teach me to seek you   11, 18
Lord, teach us to understand   95
Lord, who createdst man in wealth and store   92
Lord, you have always given   82
Loving Father, help us remember the birth of Jesus   87

May all who share these gifts today   117
May none of God's wonderful works keep silence   24
May the everlasting Father himself take you   120
May the grace of the Lord Jesus Christ   121
May the road rise up to meet you   119
May your feet walk   104
Most gracious Father   110
Most high, most powerful, good Lord   27
Move our hearts   32
My dearest Lord, be thou a bright flame before me   16
My Father, for another night   74
My Father, I abandon myself into your hands   19
My God, my God, why have you forsaken me?   54
My soul glorifies the Lord   33

Not because of your promised heaven   94
Now thank we all our God   34

O Christ, our Morning Star   75

O Divine Master, grant that I may not so much seek   22

O Father, give my spirit power to climb   17

O God of love   72

O God of peace, good beyond all that is good   66

O God our Father, we would thank you for all the bright things of life   41

O God, graciously comfort and tend all who are imprisoned   67

O God, the father of the forsaken   67

O God, the living God   61

O God, we thank you for this earth, our home   36

O God, you are my God   14

O God, you are the light of the minds that know you   15

O God, you have graciously brought us to this hour   99

O gracious and ever-living God   107

O gracious and holy Father   14

O Lamb of God   47

O Lord our God, look mercifully on us   106

O Lord, grant me to greet the coming day in peace   74

O Lord, I know not what to ask of thee   62

O Lord, thank you for bread   111

O Lord, that lends me life   35

O Lord, the day is yours, and the night is yours   73

O Lord, the Scripture says   15

O Lord, we pray for the universal church   66

O Lord, you have searched me   22

O make my heart so still, so still   20

O my divine Master   20

O my God, stand by me   56

O my Lord, I am in a dry land   60

O secret Christ   75

O you most holy and ever-loving God   74

Oh, the Lord is good to me   40

Open our hearts and minds   103

Our Father in heaven, hallowed be your name   62

Out of the depths I cry to you, O Lord   49

Pour forth, O Christ   65

Praise the Lord   26

Spirit of God, with your holy breath   99

Strengthen for service, Lord   58

Strengthen us, O God   66

Teach us, Lord   52
Thanks be to thee, my Lord Jesus Christ   39
The child of glory   90
The day thou gavest, Lord, is ended   78
The Lord bless you and keep you   119
The Lord is my shepherd   40
The Lord sanctify and bless you   107
The peace of God   121
The strife is o'er, the battle is done   94
Then let us feast this Easter Day   96
There is no place where God is not   31
There's a wideness in God's mercy   43
Therefore, if anyone is in Christ   106
This is my song, O God of all nations   64
This is that night of tears, the three days' space   94
This is the day the Lord has made   73
Thou that hast given so much to me   38
Through the Holy Spirit   100
To God the Father, who first loved us   31
To God who gives our daily bread   117
To thee, O Jesu, I direct my eyes   31

Watch, dear Lord   79
We beg you, Lord   63, 70
We beseech you, O Lord our God, be patient with us sinners   48
We give back to you, O God   113
We plough the fields, and scatter the good seed on the land   42
We pray you, Lord   88
We thank thee, Lord   52
We thank you, Father   91
We thank you, O Lord and Master   39
When I survey the wondrous cross   97
While I sleep, O Lord   76
Who goeth in the way which Christ hath gone   91
Wilt thou forgive that sin where I begun   45
Write your blessed name   57

You are holy, Lord, the only God   29
You who give food to all flesh   118
You, my God, are eternal and all-powerful   32

ACKNOWLEDGMENTS

Every effort has been made to trace and contact copyright owners for material used in this book. We apologize for any inadvertent omissions or errors, and would ask those concerned to contact us so that full acknowledgment can be made in the future.

All photographs copyright © Digital Vision, except as noted below.

pp. 16–17: Copyright © Steve Dorey/Cotswolds Photo Library.

pp. 20–21, 56–57: Copyright © Nathan Haddock.

pp. 40–41, 44–45, 72–73, 96–97, 112–13, 116–17: Copyright © Jon Arnold Images.

pp. 88–89: Copyright © Olivier Grunewald/OSF.

pp. 92–93: Copyright © FLPA/Minden.

Scripture quotations except as noted below taken from the *Holy Bible, New International Version*, copyright © 1973, 1978, 1984 International Bible Society. Used by permission of Zondervan and Hodder & Stoughton Limited. All rights reserved. The 'NIV' and 'New International Version' trademarks are registered in the United States Patent and Trademark Office by International Bible Society. Use of either trademark requires the permission of International Bible Society. UK trademark number 1448790.

p. 12: Scripture from the New Revised Standard Version published by HarperCollins Publishers, copyright © 1989 by the Division of Christian Education of the National Council of the Churches of Christ in the USA, and are used by permission. All rights reserved.

pp. 17, 69, 95: Quotations from Brother Roger are copyright © Ateliers et Presses de Taizé, 71250 Taizé-Communauté, France.

pp. 45, 47, 83, 98, 106, 107: Extracts from The Book of Common Prayer of 1662, the rights of which are vested in the Crown in perpetuity within the United Kingdom, are reproduced by permission of Cambridge University Press, Her Majesty's Printers.

pp. 55, 76, 89, 90, 91, 107, 110: Material from *The Alternative Service Book 1980* is copyright © The Central Board of Finance of the Church of England and is reproduced by permission.